THE RACE

Matt Rawlins Ph.D

Published by Green Bench Consulting Pte. Ltd &
Amuzement Publications

Cover design and layout by Kelvin Marc Tan at VERITAS. Thank you!

Editing by Pateenah Hordern, Scott Tompkins, Kay Ben-Avraham,
Douglas Oloughlin. Thank you!

The Race by Matt Rawlins

ISBN # 1-928715-37-0 (Print version)

ISBN # 1-928715-38-9 (EBook version)

Leadership Books
By Matt Rawlins

The Green Bench
A dialogue about Leadership and Change

The Green Bench II
Ongoing dialogue about Leadership
and Communication

The Lottery
A question can change a life

There's an Elephant in the Room
Discover the single most powerful tool for growth

Finding the Pain in your @ss-umption
A Leadership Tale

Uncertain Times Series:

Effective Leadership in Uncertain Times

Courageous Relationships
in Uncertain Times

Humility in Uncertain Times

HOW DO YOU
PREPARE YOURSELF
FOR THE
UNKNOWN?

A View from On Top

One evening, four friends got together to watch the sun set from the Flight Bar and Lounge at the Marina Bay Sands. It had a spectacular view of Singapore's skyline.

They had all done their Master's work together in Singapore and had become good friends. They had gone their own ways in these last years, and by some strange turn of events, all ended up in Singapore on the same weekend. They found themselves in a reflective mood as they looked over the city, slowly turning on its lights below them.

Kwan stated, "This city, my city, should not even exist. It has no natural resources and no capacity to feed itself. Fifty years ago you would have been insane to think about seeing this view before you."

Mark glanced at him, nodding. He pondered out loud, "The unknown future… unfortunately, I know that feeling well. I may lose my job because there is a new company in China that can produce a similar product as ours for half the price, and we can't compete."

May responded, "We recently lost our King in Thailand. He was a good man and served seventy years. We don't know what is going to happen next. Also my parents are getting older and I am not sure how to help them."

Esther looked at May and said, "Funny we are talking about all this, as I have been working in the financial district in London, and Brexit has shaken us to the core. We are not sure what is going to happen next, and as a result I don't know what my job will look like in a couple of years, or even if I will have one."

Mark declared, "We just elected Trump as President in the US, and no one in politics saw that coming. It is a whole new world, and the future is clearly unknown."

As they sat and watched the sun sink below the horizon and the city turned on its lights all around them, they realized they were all struggling with the same feeling. They were in different sectors, working in different nations, and yet there was this painful sense of an unknown future common to all of them.

Finally Kwan said, "To be honest, I have been fearful of the unknown recently. I have spent a few sleepless nights wondering about the future for my family, and especially for my young son. I thought if I could figure it out, I could do something about it. The reality is that I don't know what is ahead, and that terrified me. Then I heard a professor tell a simple story, and it changed everything for me."

He was silent for a moment and the others sat waiting. Finally Esther spoke up, laughing, "You always did love to draw it out as long as you could. Tell us what you heard."

Kwan smiled and said, "The professor started with a simple point: 'It is estimated that 65% of children entering primary school today will ultimately end up working in job types that aren't on the radar yet.'"

Kwan hesitated, raised his hands, and continued, "Granted, I am not in primary school, but he got my attention, and as I said, as I am deeply concerned about my son and his future. The professor then went on to ask these questions to summarize the world we are all living in:

"How do you prepare a generation for jobs that don't exist yet?

"How do you succeed in a world that is changing so fast?

"How can you strategically plan for the unknown?

"Things are changing so fast, no one knows what the future holds. Über, Google, Facebook, Twitter, Instagram, driverless cars, changing weather patterns…"

Esther jumped in quickly, "Yes, we've got all that coming at us daily in the news. We know the future is changing fast. What did you hear that helped you?"

Kwan smiled. "It is a story called The Race. The professor summarized his years of research in organizational development, strategic leadership, and dealing with the unknown, and he put it together in a unique story of how a remote village learned to survive against all the odds. Just as this isolated village had no idea how to prepare for life in a city, so each of us are faced with life in an unknown future. It gave me a way to think about my leadership and how I can prepare myself and my son for that unknown future."

He sat quietly for a minute, and Esther finally smacked his arm and stared at him meaningfully, gesturing for him to continue.

Kwan grinned. "Okay, okay. So here is the story he told that gave me understanding and hope."

The Village

There was a tribe, located high in the mountains, that took their need to train up their young people very seriously. The tribe's name was "Tiānkōng", which, when translated into English, means "sky." They were a People of the Sky. They were a ruggedly beautiful people who cared deeply about life, with a long history of rich traditions. They had deep green eyes and faces carved (with imprinted lines and deeply tanned skin) by long hours spent in the sun and wind at high altitude. The women loved bright colors, and the men tended to be more conservative.

The People of the Sky were a people who had endured great hardship over the centuries, and they fought hard for life as they eked out a living on small summer plots and herd cattle. They also wove carpets to sell with some honey and pottery. The Village was high in the mountains and had no electricity, paved roads, or schools. For water, there was a stream nearby when it rained, but the closest consistent water source was a two-hour walk away. The kids had to walk four hours to school if they wanted to go. Their interaction with the rest of the world was limited, to say the least. The building supplies for their houses were rocks pulled from the mountainside and then carried to their land. The rocks were fitted together, and then clay was put around the rocks to give them some insulation. It was back-breaking work, and all of the people knew how to work long and hard. They assumed that hard work was enough, but after their young people started failing, they knew they needed to change things.

Many years ago, they realized that many of their young people would leave The Village and go to The City, in which they would quickly be lost, as it was a completely unknown world for them. Most made it back to The Village but were often broken, addicted, or very confused. They had lost their identity and forgotten the traditions of The Village. Those that did not come back to The Village disappeared in a foreign land and were not heard from again. It seemed they had little to no skills to succeed in any Village outside their own where they grew up. It was a source of great pain to many of the families in The Village.

The Elders got together and created what they called "The Race." It started slow and eventually challenged The Village to the core. Over the course of twenty years, it grew to be a success in more ways than the Chief or Elders could have imagined. They were no longer afraid to send their young people to The City, because they knew they had some key skills needed to survive.

TOMORROW'S WORLD WILL BE
UNKNOWABLY DIFFERENT
FROM THE WORLD
YOU LIVE AND MOVE IN TODAY.

HOW DO YOU PREPARE FOR IT?

Let the Race Begin

Few families and even fewer communities would be willing to admit that their young people were not being prepared for a new world. It is an unnerving confession. The most common assumption you find in an older generation is, "If it was good enough for our fathers and us, then it is good enough for our children." There is this underlying assumption, "What got us here… will get them there."

WHEN REALITY KNOCKS AT THE
DOOR THROUGH TENSION,
WILL YOU ANSWER IT?

If ever there was a Village or community that was distant, removed, and one that The City had left behind, it was the People of the Sky.

They lived for thousands of years in isolation, in the most challenging circumstances; but they survived because they had a strong desire to live. They chose to face the tension. They would do whatever it took to engage life. This was one of their greatest challenges, and they stepped up to meet it as few Villages do.

NEVER FEAR TENSION, FOR IT IS OFTEN TIMES THE INCENTIVE NEEDED TO GET A PERSON OR VILLAGE ENGAGED TO LEARN.

The Village Comes Together

The one person that stirred it all up was the Chief's son, Raul. He had gone to The City and came back sick, with little heart or soul left in him. He represented their future and carried the identity of the people in him. He wore the feather of the future leader with great pride up until then, but after The City, he took the feather off and refused to wear it. Few people could bear to look at him without his feather.

That is when the Chief called the Elders together, and they decided to take action. They had very little; they were as poor as any Village anywhere on the earth. They all loved Raul, and if it could happen to him, then they all knew their own children were in danger. They had to do something; but what?

WHAT DO YOU DO WHEN YOU DON'T KNOW WHAT TO DO?

They called a Gathering of the whole Village. They sat in a large circle; anyone could say whatever they wanted, and everyone had to listen until the person felt like they had been heard.

It was a slow process, but as they spoke from the heart and listened, they all got a sense that something had to be done. Some of the voices that rang out were:

"Let's get all the youth to do something."

"Life is difficult; let's create a competition."

"I think it should be about learning respect and not just a reward if they do something."

"They need to learn how to think. To figure things out. So it should be about being clever, not just fast."

"They must be strong; they must learn through struggle."

There was slowly a growing agreement of heart as it took a while to share and listen to each other. Even the poorest of the poor had the same "time" as the wealthiest people alive, and they used it well.

> AN HONEST, VULNERABLE
> CONVERSATION IS
> WHERE ALL CHANGE BEGINS.

> IF YOU CAN'T TALK ABOUT IT,
> YOU CAN'T CHANGE IT.

After everyone had said everything they had to say, they sat in silence. Hours passed as they continued to sit and hold the weight of their young people's future in their hands and hearts. No one remembers how it came about, but at the end of the day, all agreed that a Race was the best idea they had. They agreed it was to be held once a year. Maybe that would instill challenge and a new way of thinking in the youth.

The only thing everyone had in The Village to race with was a donkey, as everyone had at least one for transportation. So it was agreed; The Race was established. It was born out of the desire to do something new, different, and to take a risk to find a way to help their young people look at life in a new way.

The First Race

Raul, the Chief's son, was brought in and asked to be in charge of The Race. He was to go away and think about what a person needed to survive in The City and incorporate the skills needed into The Race. (It was only years later that Raul discovered the great risk his father had taken, as some of the elders saw Raul only through his failure. Their argument was, "How could a young feather-carrier who failed ever lead?" "He gave up the feather... He is not wearing it; how can he now lead?")

For the first time in a long time, Raul had a spark in his eyes. He saw the challenge and the responsibility and took it seriously. He knew he had failed, but if he and others could learn from it, it would make it worthwhile. He had nine months to make a plan.

Raul thought long and hard about it. Years later, in a private conversation with a close friend, he explained that in those early days he couldn't really see how it would help, but because he didn't want to let his father or tribe down, he took The Race very seriously.

In the end, the first Race was a simple three kilometer race around the houses in The Village, down the valley, up the other side, and then twice more around The Village.

The prize was a one-year "ownership" of a specially-built bench above The Village that had the best view over it. It was stained green, as that was their color for significance. You could oversee the whole Village from there, and the sunsets seen from there across the mountains were stunning. The chief had spent the first nine months before The Race sitting on it at different times, and no one else was allowed to sit on it unless invited by him. The winner of The Race would win the right to the bench, and no on else could sit on it, unless invited—even the Chief had to be invited.

Also, everyone who walked to get water had to stop at the champion's house and give a four-liter container of water to the family.

FIND WAYS TO CELEBRATE
"FIRST" RISKS.

> NEVER UNDERESTIMATE
> SMALL BEGINNINGS.
> IT IS NOT THE SIZE OF
> THE BEGINNING BUT THE LEADERSHIP
> AND RISK INVOLVED THAT MATTER.

In truth, those in The Village remembered little of the first Race. It was a place to start, and few starts are very glorious. But for a change to be made, there must be a start. All the men participated; a young teenager gave it his all and won. He had nothing to lose and was tired of fetching water from the river.

One thing that stood out in the following year was that, when he would sit on his bench, people would stop and gaze at him. He had a growing sense that he was special, as he was in a place no one else could be. One day the Chief came by, greeted him, and then spoke these words: "May I sit with you on the bench for a moment?" It was those words that changed the boy into a young man, as he felt respect for the first time in his life.

RESPECT — THAT MOMENT YOU REALIZE YOUR LIFE HAS VALUE.

The most dramatic change was actually in Raul. He didn't enter The Race, as he was in charge of it, but in the simplest terms, he became curious. He had hated formal education, as he felt like a failure because he didn't think the way they taught. He was tired by the time he got to school, and others made him look stupid. As the Chief's son, it was a totally new experience to have others not care about his position, so he gave up and worked in the Village. It was safer there.

However, The Race was his. It was the first time he had ever "owned" something on his own, and it was terrifying and wonderful all at the same time. Because the goal was very clear, it gave him a way to think about The Race. He could evaluate it clearly.

> CURIOSITY IS A POWERFUL
> FUEL FOR LEARNING.

> IF PEOPLE OWN IT, THEY WILL
> TAKE RESPONSIBILITY FOR IT.

After the first Race, Raul sent the young winner, whose name was Shab, to The City. He went with him but told Shab that he would not give him any help. Shab was given a small amount of money and had to survive for one week. Shab only lasted one day; he was terrified and had no idea what to do, and he begged to go home quickly after someone cheated him out of his money and he had nothing. He wanted to go home to his bench as quickly as he could.

Raul was more shocked at his own reaction. He knew Shab would have a very hard time, but what terrified him was that he could see himself in Shab and understood how Shab felt. He was the Chief's son, and Shab was no one—and yet they experienced the same thing. Raul had to admit it had taken him longer because of his own pride, but he had had the same thing happen to him, and he'd not had any idea how to deal with it. It seemed that your status in The Village didn't transfer to The City!

Raul realized that a single race did nothing to prepare the winners for The City. He had not thought of the skills needed for survival in The City, so he went back to work to set up the next Race and see what he could change. His greatest gift at this time was that he was willing to learn.

The Second Race

Months passed, and there was excitement building as people of the Village began to talk about The Race. You could see the men out practicing how to ride their donkeys. They were also feeding the donkeys a bit more and taking better care of them. Raul watched them closely, and one day as he was out walking and thinking, he saw several young men (one was Shab) walking carefully over the racecourse with their donkeys, looking at each step. He realized they all assumed they had it all figured out, and nothing would change. It was a typical Village mentality.

As Raul later expressed it, "The whole challenge of dealing with going to The City was that everything was different there. That was the whole point of The Race."

He realized it had little to do with The City—or Village, for that matter—the real question was, how do you deal with new situations or the unknown? That was what they had to learn for The Race to be successful.

> PEOPLE OWN SOMETHING BY
> HAVING A CHOICE IN THE MATTER.
> THIS INCLUDES THE FREEDOM
> TO CHANGE IT.

Raul thought long and hard about it and felt within himself the struggle of his people. They were thinking and talking more and more about The Race as the day approached. He recognized in himself the desire to do what they expected of him. He was expected to set up The Race in the same way as last year, or they were going to be very disappointed. Now he had expectations he had to deal with. The first Race was easy because no one had any expectations, but now they had a sense of it and wanted it to be the same Race again, so they could sit on the bench and have water delivered to their house.

> OTHERS' EXPECTATIONS CAN BLIND
> US TO THE UNKNOWN.

> THEY CAN CREATE A FEAR OF
> FAILURE AND BIAS US AGAINST
> LOOKING AT LIFE IN A NEW WAY.

He was confronted with the power of disappointing those you respected and cared about. Then it struck him clearly: this emotion was a key part of learning in the unknown, and somehow he had to adapt it as a part of The Race. He thought of his failure in The City and how he had no idea how to deal with all the new feelings that came up in that time. The Village only teaches you to feel one way, but in The City, there was a whole range of feelings rarely experienced in The Village. What do you do with all these new feelings?

Raul now understood the power of expectations: how they seemed to demand relational attention and created a focus on how you "should" look at things. The second Race was actually much harder to organize, because he was confronted with how he was going to do it: change it, or do the same thing? He realized he didn't like the risk of change, as it made him feel vulnerable and exposed.

In that same moment, he realized another thing: when he went into The City the first time, these were the feelings that made him so uncomfortable, and he didn't know how to deal with them. No one had taught him or helped him understand these new feelings and what you do with them.

The first and maybe the strongest lesson he was learning was that he had to take a risk himself in leading and organizing The Race. If he didn't take a risk, how could he expect them to do so? If he didn't face his fear of not meeting their expectations, how could he expect them to face their fears?

He was seeing that "new" and "risk" were two sides of the same coin. It was his first real insight into leadership; he had to take the risk and face his fear of failure before The Village could. He decided to take the risk and stay curious.

With this decision to face his failure came the decision to wear his leadership feather again. He was learning to lead while facing his own pain.

PREPARING FOR THE UNKNOWN IS AN EMOTIONAL ISSUE.

He became excited, because he saw that The Race could help people understand risk and the new emotions that came with it. If they worked with these emotions before they got to The City, they would be far more prepared for The City. Maybe The Race was exactly what they needed as a Village to help them adapt and grow in new ways?

So Raul began planning the second Race—and changed it. It was a new route, and the contestants had to stop in the middle and stack stones one meter tall before they could continue.

Raul remembered clearly the start of the second Race. He stood up and got everyone's attention; he explained the route and the new addition of stacking the rocks. He remembered the look on Shab's face: fear, loss, and disappointment. In the first Race, Shab had nothing to lose, but this Race it changed; he thought he had everything to lose, which changed how he raced.

You could hear the murmuring going on in the crowd as they began to talk amongst themselves. They clearly didn't like what Raul did, but he stuck to his goal of using The Race to prepare people and not just doing the same thing over again and playing it safe.

It was then that Raul raised his voice to the crowd and said, "The Race is not an end in itself. It does not give us anything. It is to prepare us for the future. What can you learn from it? That is the task the Chief gave me, and that is the work for all of us."

Raul looked quickly over at his father and saw a smile lingering on his face; and he knew The Race was a gift to him as well as The Village, to prepare them for The City. He also felt respect: a feeling he had not felt in a long while.

> YOU CAN'T SURVIVE IN THE CITY
> WITHOUT TAKING A RISK.

> TAKING A RISK INVOLVES EMOTIONS
> YOU RARELY FACE IN THE VILLAGE.

The second Race was won by Luon, a senior person in the village who was slower in his donkey racing but had stacked rocks his whole life and did it so quickly that he made up the time and beat the younger ones.

Raul was so tempted to shout out to everyone around that some of the skills they had learned already would help them in The Race, but he didn't. They would have to discover it on their own in the years ahead. Their life now was not wasted, just different, and they already had some of the strengths they needed to take into The City with them.

Shab gave up his green bench to Luon, and Raul hoped that Shab would learn and grow rather than just be angry about his loss. Raul realized that only time would tell. He noted to himself that he would need to have a conversation with Shab after he got over the initial disappointment, to see how he could help him.

Raul was very disappointed when Luon would not even go to The City. Luon had gone a couple times in the past and didn't like it at all. He was content with the bench and the help with water. He wanted nothing else and didn't care about The City.

It was then that Raul realized that changing The Village was going to take some time, because what needed to change were the motivations, values, and beliefs of the people, and those were the hardest to change. Some of the older ones had no desire to learn or face The City. It was a low point for him in his work of leading The Race. He knew he needed to push them enough to get them uncomfortable and thinking, but yet not too much, or they would cut him off. He learned to carry the tension of this over the years.

New Races for the
Next Three Years

The next couple of Races went on, with each one being different.

Raul added a wall climb up the face of a steep cliff one year. A few of the older contestants tried but quickly realized there was no way up it for them, so they just sat down or walked away.

The older contestants complained, but Raul made it a part of the conversation with them each year. He gave them permission to say anything they wanted, but then he pushed back about the purpose of The Race. There were just some things in The City you couldn't do, and that was a part of the journey. Life is not fair; deal with it and move on.

He then asked them if they had asked for help from others.

"No, that wasn't a part of The Race," they would quickly say. Raul realized early on that he must make the rules very clear about what they could not do, but he left it wide open for what they could do in creative ways. He discovered that people added rules that were not in The Race to try to keep "safe."

> CREATIVITY IS A VITAL TOOL YOU HAVE IN PREPARING FOR THE CITY.

> BREAKING INTERNAL "RULES" IS A PART OF CREATIVITY.

The next year, Raul added to The Race two riddles about the history of The Village at specific stops. He realized he had heard the stories about the history of The Village but had to admit he never really listened to them. He interviewed the Elders, gathered some key pieces of their history, and put it into The Race so that those who knew the answers would know where to look for the clues to move forward.

As he explored The Village's history, he wondered that if he, the Chief's son, had not really listened to the stories, how many other people in the village didn't really listen or understand the reason for the traditions?

He asked more questions to try to capture the stories of their history and started to pull others into the conversation. He understood that unless he had a clear sense of where they came from and who they were, they would have no sense of how to move forward.

Could it be that, to survive in The City, you had to understand your own Village and who you were? He had always seen The City as completely separate from The Village, but as he studied their history, he was beginning to sense that The Village was connected to The City, because everyone in The City came from a Village. The Village was where people got their identity, not The City.

When he added the historical riddles into The Race, it was the young people's turn to complain. This opened up a door to conversations with older generations in The Village, to understand more clearly who they were and their uniqueness. For there were no other Villages like them in all the earth; each Village was unique.

Each time someone whined and complained, he listened carefully and then pushed back—asking questions to get them thinking about their own limitations and whether they were real limitations or just self-imposed.

Is it possible, Raul came to wonder, that everyone struggles with the same things?

The question is, how will we deal with it?

EVERYONE IN EVERY PLACE
STARTS OUT IN A VILLAGE.
YOU MIGHT CALL IT A FAMILY
OR A TRIBE, BUT EVERYONE
STARTS OUT THEIR LIFE IN A SMALL,
ISOLATED "VILLAGE."

EVERYONE IS CONFRONTED IN OUR
WORLD WITH GOING TO THE CITY.

The Race Continues

The Village settled into The Race that Raul gave them each year. They learned that was the nature of The Race, and like it or not, it was the reality they accepted.

Raul realized there were very specific abilities that were important, but most of the skills needed were different types of skills from those they were used to. One of the most basic skills needed was asking questions.

Could they, would they, question things? Be curious enough to explore things with a new perspective? Would they be willing to look outside the box of The Village and explore new things?

He could sense it before he could actually see it, but the curiosity needed in The Village to move forward started ever so slowly to creep into the young people in The Village. Even some of the older ones raised questions about things that had never been talked about before.

One young person questioned their diet and the way they prepared food. She was interested in trying a new way she heard about from a friend who had gone to The City.

Another young person questioned why they tattooed men at a certain age and what it meant.

There was a bubbling curiosity seeping into The Village. It started to change some of the conversations and began to give people a bit of ease in the uncertainty. Newness didn't terrify people as it might have in the past. They seemed a bit more open to it and were willing to explore or "try on" new thoughts and then look at themselves in the Village "mirror" and talk about it.

Most people didn't even recognize it was happening, but Raul did. He was now very curious about everything and watched the people to see what was happening and how they were beginning to change their interactions with each other.

Visits to The City with Winners

Transference of skills was a major challenge, as Raul saw it. The first years, all those who went to The City had no idea how to transfer the skills of The Race to surviving in The City. It was like they learned something for one place and had no idea how to take what they learned and use it in another place.

He looked within himself and realized he was the same way. It had been the recent risks he took in leadership that opened the door to reflection, standing back from his life, being curious, being responsible: accepting who you were, but not being content with it. All these things he was bringing into The Race. He began to realize these things were also needed for life in The Village.

During one meeting, Raul suggested that they ask themselves, "How can what I learn in The Race help me succeed in The City?"

He paused, then said, "Or a better question might be: How can I live my life in The Village to help me succeed in The City?"

The Village needed to be the place transformed, and then they would not fear The City. Raul realized after the fifth or sixth Race that the problem wasn't really The City. The truth was, The City only revealed the problem that was in them already. It didn't create anything new in them; it just gave them a chance to see themselves in a new way.

> THE PROBLEM WAS ACTUALLY IN THE VILLAGE. IF PEOPLE COULD ADAPT, GROW, AND CHANGE IN THE VILLAGE, THEN THE CITY WOULD BE A NATURAL OUTGROWTH AND NOT THAT DIFFICULT.

The Tenth Race

One Race stood out to Raul like few others. He had just recently been to The City and saw women owning businesses and read about them in leadership roles. He knew in The Village that women had a very specific, clear, and limited role. He found himself asking: what if their view of women needed to change?

That year, in celebration of their Tenth Race, he announced that women would be allowed into The Race. He was shocked, as he had clearly underestimated what The Village's response would be. He was almost dragged before the Chief and the Elders, who demanded that he change it back.

That weekend, a Gathering was called in the Village. It was a long argument with a lot of tension woven through the dialogue. It challenged them to the core as a Village. Raul simply shared that women in The City had different roles, and it was something they would be confronted with there. "So let's begin to deal with it here," he said. Some of the statements made in the arguments included:

"Women have a place in our society, and it must not be changed."

"This is the way we have always done things."

"If we give them permission to move outside of their assigned roles, it will affect the families, and men will not be respected."

The Chief listened carefully to the argument, as it was heated at different moments. When at last silence fell, he said, "Do we have to do everything they do in The City? No. But we do have to agree on the reason or value we will live by and talk about it."

He then did the almost unthinkable and asked a senior woman, whose husband had been an elder in the tribe before he died, to speak for the women.

She thought carefully for several moments and then in a soft voice said, "I can only say that it would not cause us to respect you less as men—we would respect you more. To give us a choice to respect you rather than 'making' us respect you would be a higher honor for you."

It seemed it was a thought that not one man in the room had ever thought before, as silence hung in the room like a blanket over them all.

Finally, the Chief spoke up. "We have given The Race to Raul to use to prepare us for The City. It is his choice, and we will stick with it. It seems in The City our young people will be confronted with this, as it is already a fact of life there. We may want to make The City conform to our Village, but we know that will never happen.

"The Village should be a safe place to talk about anything. Let us learn how to do this and still maintain our way of life, and we will not lose those traditions we choose to keep that are important to us."

After much heartfelt thought and reflection, Raul told the women they could be in The Race if they wanted to—that he respected them to make the best choice. It was up to them.

That year, the women chose not to do The Race, but they all learned a very important lesson that stayed with them for years. If you take away people's choice, you rob them of their humanity and the ability to survive in The City. If you give them the choice and honestly share your concerns with them, many times people will surprise you, in a good way.

IN ORDER FOR PEOPLE TO VALUE
AND KEEP TRADITIONS, THEY
MUST HAVE THE FREEDOM TO
REJECT THEM. THE POWER IS IN
GIVING PEOPLE THE CHOICE.

IF THERE ARE NO CHOICES GIVEN
IN THE VILLAGE, THEN THE
CHOICES REQUIRED IN THE CITY
WILL BE OVERWHELMING.

In later years, women slowly joined The Race, and it was okay. Most of the people accepted it as a part of life and learned to live with it. Of course, the older generation had strong feelings against it, but others asked them, "Do you want your children to fail or be successful when they go to The City?"

THE PROBLEM IS INSIDE US. THE GREATEST CHALLENGE IS OVERCOMING THE LIMITATIONS OUR VILLAGE TAUGHT US GROWING UP.

Changing the Focus of
the Gatherings.

The people in the Gathering talked mostly about what they did and what happened in the past. They loved to tell and hear stories of what was. Raul began to talk in the meetings about the future and what might be: not what he wanted, but asking what they wanted.

The older ones said they just wanted for their children to be safe and to succeed.

There was no shortcut. They had to talk, to spend hours talking, and Raul understood that they were already prepared for this, as it was a normal part of Village life. The Gathering was a place where people could disagree with each other and then learn how to talk about it as a way to keep peace in The Village.

Raul realized that people only knew who they were in the past but had no idea who they could be in the future. What should the next generation keep that was a part of them, that non-negotiable "value"? For it was more of a heart issue than a behavioral issue. Could it be that most people didn't know the "why" or the value of the tradition that would help them go into the future? Raul reflected and realized that possibly the primary purpose of a tradition was that it represented what to take with them into the future.

During this season of time, Raul searched deeply into their rich traditions and heritage. For the first time in his life, they came alive to him. They weren't just old stories, but things The Village learned that was the DNA of their story as a people.

He began to push more and more dialogue at the Gatherings to have the Elders talk about who the People of the Sky were. What made The Village different from other Villages?

At first the Elders got upset at him for asking so many questions.

He asked them, "When I go into The City, how will people know I am from our tribe, our Village?

"They will see your clothes and know you are from here."

"So clothes make us who we are?"

Raul gave them this illustration. He pulled out a rock, gave it to them, and asked, "Where is this rock from? It has no clothes."

All of the Elders had worked with rocks their whole lives and understood all the different types around The Village. They each held it only for a minute, and finally the Chief said, "It is a rock from the water at the base of the Tiānkōng Hill."

"How do you know this?" Raul asked.

"We know it because the water has smoothed it and taken away all the jagged edges, the color, the veins running through the rock. We just know it."

"So how do people know us?" Raul asked. "What makes us unique so that they will say with respect about us, 'These are people from the Sky!'"

The Elders had no answer; each knew of each other and would immediately know the tribe, but they had never put it into words.

> IF YOU CAN'T PUT INTO WORDS
> WHAT IS MOST PRECIOUS TO YOU,
> THEN YOU WILL LOSE IT IN
> THE CITY, BECAUSE WHAT YOU
> CAN'T DEFINE, YOU CAN'T KEEP.

This began long conversations about what made them unique, set them apart, and helped them be clear about who they were—and who they were not and never would be.

Old stories were told over and over, as they had a renewed sense of who the leaders were in the past and how they overcame obstacles. Gradually a sense developed of how the people could personally carry their stories into the future. Raul discovered that this also made The Village much stronger and able to handle more tension, as they learned to trust each other more.

Raul understood that dialogue from the heart was a vital part of preparation for The City. To be able to hear others, to listen, to share your point, and to learn to carry the tension of The Village, was just as important as The Race in preparing people for The City. It was these times of sharing that made The Race a learning event rather than a competition. As they did this, they also discovered that their deepening relationships were a rich and rewarding part of The Village and their uniqueness. Raul had a growing awareness that deep relationships, linked to a common history, created the "bones" for all Village life.

The First Success

It was twelve years into The Race when The Village made the turn. Raul realized he could have seen it earlier if he had known what to look for, but it was all so new. One of the young winners of The Race had gone to The City and survived a week without too many problems. He was curious and had gone to the University there and asked about animals. He didn't know it, but a new idea was planted. He realized you could breed animals from other Villages. He also discovered there were new types of hybrid plants that grow better in the high mountains.

Many of the people in The Village began to realize that everything in life was training for The Race, and that no matter what job they did, it might help them in The Race. Slowly, everything done in The Village mattered. That one seed of thought transformed The Village.

Sabu was a hard-working woman with a family. This year, she quietly began to build a wall of rocks across the dry stream-bed on a leveled-out part of the slope. Others asked her what she was doing, and she would just say, "Experimenting." When rain came a couple of weeks later, the water was collected in the pond she created (she had built a dam), and the water stayed there a couple of weeks.

The people gathered around it and stared at it. A small risk—a change in the river to create a dam to hold water—saved them hours of walking. It was really a small thing in one sense, but in another, it changed hundreds of years of living in The Village and pushed them to look at the world around them in a new way.

Raul brought it up at the next Gathering and it was a wonderfully awkward conversation. Raul had learned that they must talk about everything and no matter how awkward, they needed to put words to it so they could continue to learn and grow into it.

When Raul looked back, he noticed that people were using rocks in new ways to build stairs and design more fuel-efficient fireplaces with chimneys, as they learned less smoke in the house gave them better health.

New seeds were brought in and tried in new ways for the brief growing season. Change came to be considered the norm, if such a thing is possible.

Solar cells took root in The Village. They soon had some electricity.

They made mesh "curtains" on the top of the hill to catch the moisture in the rolling clouds and fog and give them dripping access to clean water.

New breeds of chickens laid more eggs.

The Village continued to raise many questions about how they would live. Technology seemed to change monthly, but in a very real sense, they were prepared, because they had learned to talk deeply about the issues and were not afraid of taking a risk when it matched their values. They were comfortable in their own skin, so to speak, and their relationships were strong.

VILLAGES DON'T CHANGE BY THEMSELVES. SOMEONE HAS TO BE CURIOUS ENOUGH TO TAKE A RISK AND FACE THEIR FEARS IN ORDER TO CHANGE A VILLAGE INTO A CITY.

In a very strange turn of events, The Village discovered that new families wanted to join. It became another tension-filled dilemma for The Village to talk about.

In the past, there were families or individuals who joined The Village temporarily, though it was rare in their history. Often it was as the result of war, fire, or some other natural disaster that people would join them, and usually these people would leave just as soon as other options could be found.

With the adaptations, growth, and changes they had had, other Villages saw what they were doing and either wanted to join them and be a part of their community or to come and learn from them. A shocking realization at The Village Gathering was that others might view them as a City—although truth be told, most laughed at the idea.

> ANYTIME THERE IS A GREATER
> DESIRE FOR GROWTH, LEARNING,
> AND CREATIVITY THAN
> THERE IS FOR BOUNDARIES, LAWS,
> AND LIMITATIONS,
> YOU ARE IN THE PROCESS
> OF BUILDING A CITY
> THAT WILL DRAW PEOPLE
> FROM VILLAGES TO JOIN YOU.

Different experiments were tried over the years. They tried a children's Race in addition to the adult Race. It was much simpler but got the kids thinking about it much earlier in life. They tried running without the donkeys and always added new events in The Race to push them out of their comfort zone.

One day, one of the young people asked Raul what was one mistake that stood out to him as he looked back over the last twenty years. Raul asked for a day to think about it and then the next day told her that a mistake he made in the early years was thinking that everyone had to "change" to want to go to The City. It was only after looking at it over time that he realized that he only needed around 20% of the people to learn, knowing that the other 80% would follow. Some people were not made for The City. They were Village people at heart, and they were what brought the stability and "normalcy" to The Village. It gave him freedom to think that he didn't have to change everyone—just the key people who had a natural inclination towards it.

YOU CAN TURN A VILLAGE
INTO A CITY BY GETTING
20% OF THE PEOPLE INNOVATING
AND WORKING TOGETHER.

The Village Today

It is not unusual to see Raul wandering around the Village and even going to talk to other Villages nearby to hear their stories and get to know them. When he comes back from these visits, there is a curious sparkle in his eyes as he thinks of the future. He gets excited as he thinks of the possibility of new Races with other Villages and building a stronger community in the region. He would be the first to tell you he does not know what the future holds, but he is not afraid of it, for he knows it can only teach them new things.

> HE REALIZED HIS GOAL,
> THE FOCUS OF THE RACE,
> WAS TO GET THE VILLAGE TO
> VIEW LIFE AS AN OPPORTUNITY,
> A CHANCE TO LEARN AND GROW,
> AND NOT SOMETHING TO BE
> FEARED AND FRAMED AS A
> COMPETITION THAT YOU CAN "LOSE"

A Village Epilogue

As stories go, there is one more insight that must be told, for it became a vital foundation for Raul, his leadership, his understanding of The Village, and preparing for The City. I will let him tell the story himself, as it is a story only he can tell.

"It was a season of deep reflection for me, with much tension and many challenges. My father had just died, and though he was buried with his Feather of Glory and wore his Chief's robe, I remember most clearly that he left with no earthly possessions but our love.

"In the same week, my third son was born, and the image of my father passing and my son being welcomed into this world with open arms of love captured my imagination. Naked we come from our mother's womb, and naked we shall depart.

"I was also thinking about The Race. I thought of our winners; so many times, they would win, and then their fear of losing would creep in, and they would not win again for years. For whatever reason, I thought of this as "being poor."

"I was outside, as I love to be, sitting before the fire, watching the sparks rise to the stars above, an intimate chill in the air, and listening to my wife snore gently in the house.

"I was wrestling with how poor we were as a Village, and with the ache I felt in my heart. Then somehow, all these images of dying naked and being born naked, yet wrapped in love, brought insight to me that I do not know how to put clearly in words. We are not poor; that just describes our possessions. All humanity brings nothing with them into the world and can take nothing with us out of it. We have love, and that matters more than the possessions. It is often our poverty that makes us hungry and willing to work hard and take the risks needed.

"It was a moment in time that changed my view of who I am, my leadership, who The Village is, and how I view The City. Poverty, having less, going without: all of these can be a blessing. It keeps life simple, and being simple is often a great way you can learn about love, relationships, and how to survive in The City. In essence, I don't even fear poverty any more, for it has things to teach me. I guess what I fear most is not having love and not learning."

THE LESS YOU HAVE TO WORRY
ABOUT, THE MORE YOU CAN LIVE
A SIMPLER LIFE, WHICH MAKES
LEARNING EASIER, AS THERE MAY
BE LESS "LOSS" LINKED TO IT.

LESS CAN BE MORE.

Singapore: A New View

With that, Kwan finished his story, and the four friends sat quietly as they thought about the story and how it seemed to come alive before them as they looked at the city of Singapore. The wind picked up on the 57th floor as the heavy, humid air pushed its way around.

Kwan said, "It is strange to repeat that story while sitting and overlooking a city-nation that shouldn't even exist. Our leader is gone, and my family and friends are trying to figure out what the next fifty years look like, and truthfully, nobody knows. I am pretty sure they don't like the feeling. I know I don't."

Kwan was silent for a moment and then continued, "We were a Village that was kicked out of Malaysia and left to die. No one thought we could make it, and now look at us. The Village of Singapore woke up one day and realized: we are a world-class City, and now we don't know what to do with it. Personally, I can see myself in this story. I identify with Raul and his struggles. It has changed my thinking in how I work with people around me, and especially with my son."

Mark nodded. "Even if you are born into a City like Singapore, you still view it as a Village, because you grew up there. Now the next generation needs to rethink how to lead into the unknown, and that means taking a risk to try some new things."

May reflected, "I see it applies for my beloved Thailand as well. What will we be as a nation without our cherished King? I might also add that I come from a Village near Chiang Mai, and I can identify with that story. I thought I outgrew the Village, but now I realize I didn't. I can see what I learned applies to my life today and even to my country. I need to rethink my view of leadership and not think like a technical manager, as my MBA taught me, but more like a Village leader preparing for The City. It might sound odd, but I can do that."

Esther reached over, took her hand, and said, "You have a strength that I love. You have already done it just by being here." She hesitated and then continued, "On a personal note, I can see that I have feared the changes from Brexit and my getting fired, and I have stopped learning. I have been living in fear of the unknown, and I can see it in my own leadership. I limited my learning to my MBA and forgot it was about life."

Mark nodded in agreement. "I hear ya, sister. I think I failed my 'learning exam' after school... you know, that exam you called 'life.' I have let others' expectations and my own fears kill my capacity to be curious and take risks."

The four new students of life sat and looked over the city below them, deep in thought. They realized they needed to make some changes and needed help.

Kwan finally said, "How about this: we start a learning group, just like school. Instead of calling it a Gathering, how about we call it 'Cheem'? That is a Singlish word which loosely translated means confounding, confusing or complex. In our group, we share honestly; we listen and push each other in our leadership. We take some new risks. We create a place to connect, a place to talk about The Race we are in, and what we can learn. What do you think?"

Mark smiled. "A new tribe is born. We are the 'People of the Cheem.' I like it."

The smiles on all their faces as they looked at each other confirmed it. A new Village was born that would help them figure out a path to a new City.

One Year Later

It has been a year, and the friends set up a private chat group. With calls, connections at airports, and time together to enjoy great meals, they continued the journey together.

As any Village should do, they tracked their story and gathered the key points that they wanted to be a part of their People of the *Cheem* "traditions." They wanted others to learn from their Race, and so these traditions are included below.

Yours will be different, as each Village is different, but it gives you a starting point in your own journey to The City. Have a good trip, and remember: the journey is just as important as the arrival. On your way, take love with you.

People of
the *Cheem*

**OUR
TRADITIONS**

GET TO KNOW YOURSELF; BE COMFORTABLE IN YOUR OWN SKIN.

Don't try to be all things to all people.
You have strengths and weaknesses;
embrace them, and use your strengths
as often as you can.

What do you value that is a core part of
your motivation in life?

How can you defend these values in a
healthy way?

It is only when you know what you value
that you can let go of the things that are
not that important.

Find ways to challenge yourself to
step out of the box (Village) and try
something new. Pay close attention to
the emotions that rise up during this
process.

Work at being "Fully Present." Be aware
of what diminishes you and face it.

Remember to keep the most
importantthing the most important.

BE AWARE OF YOUR EMOTIONS.

The battle to prepare for The City begins
within you.

Start within, now, and let it work
its way out.

Values communicate through feelings.
Name the feelings, put words to them,
and own them. They are yours.

Talk with those around you about what
you value.

Create dialogue to practice putting words
to your values. Include your joys and fears
(emotions) in this dialogue.

Never underestimate the power of
emotional words. Use them wisely.

Don't let your feelings keep you from
taking the risks you need to succeed.

You may need to let go of something old
to get something new.

TENSION IS A FRIEND

Work with tension; embrace it, and don't react to it.

Tension is a gift, a signal that things are not as expected.

Tension's purpose is to raise questions. Be extra careful what questions you ask; the question you ask directs your attention.

Tension also reveals emotions in you; own them and work with them.

You can't go where you want to go without tension and risk. It is vital to City Life.

KEEP IT SIMPLE

Sometimes, the less you have to carry
and move, the freer you are to learn
and innovate.

More is not always better. You are not
poor if you have "less."

You must take love from The Village with
you into The City. If you can't find it in
The Village, it will be almost impossible
to find in The City.

You must give love to make space for it
in your own life.

The hardest discipline in any community
is to keep it simple.

THE CITY IS WHERE PEOPLE
GO TO FLEE A VILLAGE THAT
WON'T CHANGE.

IF YOU ARE NOT TAKING A RISK
RIGHT NOW IN YOUR VILLAGE,
YOU WILL NOT BE ABLE TO FACE
THE CITY; IT IS THAT SIMPLE.
IT BEGINS RIGHT NOW, RIGHT
WHERE YOU ARE.

About the Author

Unabashed in his pointed questions and unrelenting in his encouragement for those around him to live a life of integrity, Dr. Matthew Rawlins is a passionate educator and brilliant communicator in both speech and writing. He has been invited to lecture in over 35 nations, and has published 15 books. He gained his Ph.D. in communication and leadership development through the University of Wales, and currently is CEO of Green Bench Consulting in Singapore. His work focuses on difficult conversations in organizational change, leadership, and conflict. He also does executive coaching.

He will help you get from The Village to The City.

If you are interested in bulk orders of this book or have questions, please contact Matt at:
Email: mrawlins@mac.com
Company website is: thegreenbench.com
Facebook: Green Bench Consulting
                     The Race